D1146049

Will Shortz Presents

THE LITTLE GIFT BOOK OF KENKEN

KenKen: Logic Puzzles That Make You Smarter!

Will Shortz Presents KenKen Easiest, Volume 1
Will Shortz Presents KenKen Easy, Volume 2
Will Shortz Presents KenKen Easy to Hard, Volume 3
Will Shortz Presents The Little Gift Book of KenKen

KenKen for Kids

Will Shortz Presents I Can KenKen! Volume 1
Will Shortz Presents I Can KenKen! Volume 2
Will Shortz Presents I Can KenKen! Volume 3

WILL SHORTZ PRESENTS

THE LITTLE GIFT BOOK OF KENKEN

250 LOGIC PUZZLES THAT MAKE YOU SMARTER

Created by
TETSUYA MIYAMOTO

ST. MARTIN'S GRIFFIN
NEW YORK

The puzzles in this volume have previously appeared in *Will Shortz Presents KenKen Easiest*, Volume 1; *Will Shortz Presents KenKen Easy*, Volume 2; *Will Shortz Presents KenKen Easy to Hard*, Volume 3.

WILL SHORTZ PRESENTS THE LITTLE GIFT BOOK OF KENKEN. Puzzle content copyright © 2008 by Gakken Co., Ltd. Introduction copyright © 2008 by Will Shortz. All rights reserved. Printed in the United States of America. For information, address St. Martin's Press, 175 Fifth Avenue, New York, N.Y. 10010.

www.stmartins.com

ISBN-13: 978-0-312-55851-2
ISBN-10: 0-312-55851-1

First Edition: October 2008

10   9   8   7   6   5   4   3   2   1

Introduction

If you consider all the world's greatest puzzle varieties, the ones that have inspired crazes over the years—crosswords, jigsaw puzzles, tangrams, sudoku, etc.—they have several properties in common. They . . .

- Are simple to learn
- Have great depth
- Are variable in difficulty, from easy to hard
- Are mentally soothing and pleasing
- Have some unique feature that makes them different from everything else and instantly addictive

By these standards, a new puzzle called KenKen, the subject of the book you're holding, has the potential to become one of the world's greats.

KenKen is Japanese for "square wisdom" or "cleverness squared."

The rules are simple: Fill the grid with digits so as not to repeat a digit in any row or column (as in sudoku) and so the digits within each heavily outlined group of boxes combine to make the arithmetic result indicated.

KenKen puzzles start with 3×3 boxes and use only addition. Harder examples have larger grids and more arithmetic operations.

KenKen was invented in 2003 by Tetsuya Miyamoto, a Japanese math instructor, as a means to help his students learn arithmetic and develop logical thinking. Tetsuya's education method is unusual. Put simply, he doesn't teach. His philosophy is to make the tools of learning available to students and then let them progress on their own.

Tetsuya's most popular learning tool has been KenKen, which his students spend hours doing and find more engaging than TV and video games.

It's true that KenKen has great capacity for educating and building the mind. But first and foremost it's a puzzle to be enjoyed. It is to numbers what the crossword puzzle is to words.

So turn the page and begin. . . .

—Will Shortz

How to Solve KenKen

KenKen is a logic puzzle with simple rules:

- Fill the grid with digits so as not to repeat a digit in any row or column.
- Digits within each heavily outlined group of squares, called a cage, must combine to make the arithmetic result indicated.
- A 3×3–square puzzle will use the digits from 1 to 3, a 4×4–square puzzle will use the digits from 1 to 4, etc.

Solving a KenKen puzzle involves pure logic and mathematics. No guesswork is needed. Every puzzle has a unique solution.

In this volume of KenKen, there are five types of KenKen puzzles: puzzles that use addition only, multiplication only, addition and subtraction, multiplication and division, and finally puzzles that use all four arithmetic operations—addition, subtraction, multiplication, and division.

In a cage marked with a plus sign, the given number will be the sum of the digits you enter in the squares. In a cage marked with a minus sign, the given number will be the difference between the digits you enter in the squares (the lower digit subtracted from the higher one). Similarly, in a cage marked with a times or division sign, the given number will be the product or quotient, respectively, of the digits you enter in the squares (for division, the higher digit divided by the lower one).

Here is an example of how to solve an addition-only KenKen puzzle.

9+	4	3+		1−
	8+		1	
2	4−	1−		9+
2−		6+	3	
	2		4−	

To start, fill in the digits in the 1×1 cages—the 4 in the top row, the 1 in the second row, etc. This puzzle has five such isolated squares. They are literally no-brainers.

Next, look for cages whose given numbers are either high or low, since these are often the easiest to solve. For example, the top row has a cage with a sum of 3. The only two digits that add up to 3 are 1 and 2. The 1 can't go in the fourth column, because this column already has a 1. So the 1 must go in the third column. The 2 goes next to it in the fourth column.

Similarly, check out the cage in the first column with a sum of 9. The only two digits from 1 to 5 that add up to 9 are 4 and 5. The 4 can't go in the top row, because this row already has a 4. So it must go in the second row. The 5 goes above it in the first row.

Sometimes the next step in solving a KenKen puzzle is to ignore the given numbers and use sudoku-like logic to avoid repeating a digit in a row or column.

For example, the first column in our sample puzzle starts out 5, 4, and 2. The bottom two squares must be 1 and 3, in some order. (They do indeed have a difference of 2, as shown.) The 3 can't go in the fourth row, because this row already has a 3. So it must go in the fifth row, with the 1 going immediately above it.

Continuing in this way, using these and other techniques left for you to discover, you can work your way around the grid, filling in the rest of the squares. The complete solution is shown below.

9+ 5	4 4	3+ 1	2	1− 3
4	8+ 3	5	1 1	2
2 2	4− 1	1− 3	4	9+ 5
2− 1	5	6+ 2	3 3	4
3	2 2	4	4− 5	1

Additional Notes

- In advanced KenKen puzzles, cages can have more than two squares. It's okay for a cage to repeat a digit—as long as the digit is not repeated in a row or column.
- Cages with more than two squares will always involve addition or multiplication. Subtraction and division occur only in sections with exactly two squares.
- Remember, in doing KenKen, you never have to guess. Every puzzle can be solved by using step-by-step logic. Keep going, and soon you'll be a KenKen master!

+ **1**

3	3	
6		
5		1

2 +

3	4	
	5	3
3		

+ **3**

5	**3**	
	3	**4**
3		

4 +

3	5	1
		5
4		

+/− **5**

1−	**4**+	
	1	**5**+
3+		

6 +/−

3	1−	
3+		5+
2−		

$\times$ **7**

3	6	3
		2
2		

8 ×

3		2
6	2	
	3	

$\times$ **9**

2		3
3	2	
	6	

10 ×

2		3
3	6	
	2	

×/÷   **11**

2÷		3
6×	2×	
	3×	

12 ×/÷

3×	6×	1
		6×
2÷		

+/−/×/÷ **13**

2	3÷	
4+		1−
6×		

14   +/−/×/÷

5+		**2−**
2÷		
1	**6×**	

+ **15**

4		6	
7	3	4	
		3	7
6			

16 +

1	7		3
7	3	3	
	3		7
2		4	

+ **17**

5	5		4
	5	5	
3		5	3
5			

18 +

7	2	3	4
	7		3
3		3	
	5		3

+ **19**

6			9
3	1	7	
	7		
4		3	

20 +

5	5	6	
		5	1
5	1		7
	5		

+ 21

9		3	
	3	5	
6	5		4
		5	

22 +

4	2	7	
	5	3	5
6			
	7		1

+ **23**

5		3	3
4	5	3	
5			4
	1	7	

24 +

3	7		5
	3	4	
7		5	
	3	3	

+ **25**

5		**5**	
8	**3**		**7**
	5		
	7		

26 +

4	7		6
	3		
6	4	3	
		7	

+ **27**

7		3	7
	5	3	
3			7
5			

28 +

6	7		6
	4		
		4	6
7			

+ **29**

3	7	7	
7		1	
	6		5
	4		

30 +

3	5	3	
5		2	7
	2	7	
5			1

+ **31**

9	6		
	3	5	
		9	
8			

32 +

3	7	4	
		7	3
6			
4		6	

+ **33**

3	7	8	3
3			
	2		7
7			

34 +

8	9		
	3	4	
		3	7
6			

+ **35**

6		7	3
3	7		
		4	
4		6	

36 +

7			5
5		6	
7	5		
		5	

+ **37**

3	3		7
3	1	7	
	7		2
4		3	

38 +

7	8		
	5		9
	8	3	

+ **39**

5	5		4
	3	4	
5		4	3
	7		

40 +/−

3+	7+		1−
	3−		
9+		2−	
	7+		

+/− **41**

3	**1**−		**7**+
3+	**9**+		
		5+	
4	**1**−		**1**

42 +/−

3−	5+	4+	
		2−	
2−		1−	7+
6+			

2−	**3**+		**7**+
	1−	**7**+	
6+			
	3−		**3**

44 +/−

5+		3−	
3+	5+		1−
	1−		
7+		1−	

46 +/−

1	7+	3	3+
1−		1−	
	3+		4
2		7+	

+/− **47**

6+	9+	1−	
		7+	
		2−	4+
3−			

48 +/−

7+	3−		5+
	3+	1−	
3+			5+
	7+		

+/− **49**

6+			4
7+	7+	2−	
			3+
2	1−		

50 +/−

6+	11+		1−
		4+	
			8+
2−			

+/−   **51**

8+			7+
7+		7+	
6+			
		1−	

52 +/−

1−		11+	
9+	2−		
	3−	3+	
		1−	

+/− **53**

1−	8+		
	9+		1−
12+			
		3−	

54 ×

2	12		3
4	1	6	
	8		4
3		2	

$\times$ **55**

1	12		2
12	2	6	
	4		12
2		1	

56 ×

12	6		
	12		24
	4	4	

$\times$ **57**

4	2	2	3
	12		4
6		3	
	4		2

58 ×

8	4	3	
	2	4	6
3			
	6		4

$\times$ **59**

12	4		6
	6	2	
2			4
	12		

60 ×

8	12		1
	4	6	
3		1	8
	6		

$\times$ **61**

4	12		2
	6		
2		4	12
6			

62 ×

6	4		2
	12	3	
1		2	12
8			

× **63**

6	8		4
	4	3	
4		6	
	3	2	

64 ×

24			6
2	3	4	
	4		
3		8	

$\times$ **65**

3	2	4	
2		4	6
	4	6	
12			1

66 ×

6		1	12
	2	12	
4			4
12			

$\times$ **67**

1	3	8	
6		2	12
	4		
8		3	

68 ×

1	4	18	
24		4	
	6		4
	2		

$\times$ **69**

12		4	2
6			
4	2	12	
		6	

70 ×

3		4	8
3	4	2	
8			3
	2	3	

$\times$ **71**

6		4	
4		6	12
3	8		
		2	

72 ×

6			4
12		12	
2	4		
		12	

$\times$ **73**

8	12		
	12	6	8
3			
	2		

74 ×

4	**2**	**12**	**6**
2			
	3		**4**
24			

$\times$ **75**

2		12	
	4	6	
24	6		1
		4	

76 ×

9	2		32
8	6		3
	4		

$\times$ **77**

6		4	
12	4		6
	2		
	24		

78 ×

6	12		
	8	4	
		6	
24			

2÷		12×	1
12×	1		6×
	2÷		
1	6×		4

80 ×/÷

2÷	2÷		12×
	12×		
72×			
		2÷	

×/÷ **81**

3	16×		2÷
2÷		3	
	6×		12×
8×			

82   ×/÷

2÷	48×		6×
	6×		
24×			4×

×/÷ **83**

2÷	24×		
	12×	4×	
12×			6×
	2÷		

84 ×/÷

12×		24×	
6×		2×	
	2÷		
		12×	

8×		**12×**	
3×			**8×**
12×		**12×**	

86 ×/÷

12×	2÷		2÷
	12×		
	3	2÷	
2÷		12×	

1	12×	6×	
2÷		2÷	
	2÷	4	12×
3			

88 ×/÷

6×	2÷		48×
12×		2÷	
	24×		

2÷		12×	
12×	12×		8×
	6×		
		2÷	

90 ×/÷

8×			12×
12×		12×	
12×			
		2÷	

2÷	2÷		12×
	2÷	12×	
36×			2÷

92 ×/÷

7+	2÷		1−
	4+		
2÷		6×	1−
3−			

94   +/−/×/÷

4+		**3**+	**4**
2	**8**×		**3**×
4×		**3**	
	12×		**2**

+/−/×/÷ **95**

7+		**6×**	**1−**
3−			
2÷	**1−**	**4÷**	
		12×	

96 +/−/×/÷

6×	1	6+	
	8×	1	3×
4		7+	
4+			2

+/−/×/÷　97

4+	2÷	3−	
		7+	6×
1−			
24×			

98 +/−/×/÷

6+	1	7+	
	3×		2
4×		2	4+
3	8×		

2÷	12×		
	3+		36×
2−	6+		
		1−	

100 +/−/×/÷

2	7+		4+
6+		1	
3×	1	8×	
	5+		4

5+	3	8×	
	6+	3×	3
2			2÷
2−		4	

102 +/−/×/÷

9+		6+	
	12×		
6×		48×	

4	3+		3
4+	6×		8×
	5+	12×	
2			1

104 +/−/×/÷

3+	**7**+		**1**
	2÷	**1**−	
12×		**1**	**6**×
	2÷		

2	5+		3
12×	2÷		3−
	7+	6×	
1			2

106 +/−/×/÷

2÷	**7**+		**1**
	2÷		**5**+
1−		**1**	
1−		**12**×	

+/−/×/÷ **107**

2÷		1−	
3−	1−		1−
	5+		
5+		5+	

108 +/−/×/÷

6+			12×
8×	3−	7+	
			2÷
	6×		

+/−/×/÷ 109

12×	**3÷**		**2×**
	1−	**2÷**	
1−			**7+**
	6+		

110 +/−/×/÷

4+		2÷	12×
6+			
3−	6×	2−	
		2÷	

2×	12×		2
	1	7+	
12×	6×		1
	2	5+	

112 +/−/×/÷

1−		5+	
2÷		12×	
7+	2÷		1−
	4+		

8+	24×		
	7+		12×
		3−	
2÷			

114 +/−/×/÷

3−		**5+**	
3÷	**2**	**12×**	
	2÷		**5+**
2	**2−**		

+/−/×/÷ **115**

3−		5+	
9+			12×
6×	2÷		
	5+		

116 +/−/×/÷

2	12×		2÷
7+		1	
5+	2	1−	
	3+		3

7+			9+
5+		2−	
12×	1−		
		2÷	

118 +/−/×/÷

2	7+		3÷
12×	3+		
	4÷		2
4+		8×	

2÷		48×	
4+	1−		
	7+		5+
12×			

120 +/−/×/÷

18×		**16×**	**1−**
5+	**2÷**	**5+**	
		1−	

+/−/×/÷ 121

7+		**2÷**	
3+	**2÷**		**12×**
	2−		
1−		**5+**	

122 +/−/×/÷

3−		72×	
2÷	9+		
			1−
8+			

+/−/×/÷ **123**

2−	5+		2÷
	72×		
8×			6+

124 +/−/×/÷

5+	**1−**		**12×**
	3−	**7+**	
4÷			**2÷**
	6×		

96×	2÷		1−
		6+	
	6×		
		1−	

126 +/−/×/÷

5+	3	2÷	
	6×		1
4+		2	12×
2	3−		

4	12×	2−	
2÷			3−
	11+		
4+			2

128 +/−/×/÷

7+			2−
12×		2	
	4	24×	
6×			

+/− 129

1−		**9**+		**1**
2	**4**−	**7**+		**1**−
6+		**3**	**1**−	
	4	**3**+		**5**+
7+			**5**	

130 +/−

1	2−		10+	
1−	6+	14+		
			2−	
3−		1−		9+
	2−			

1–	4+		1–	5
	7+			1–
9+	3–		2	
	9+	4+		3+
3		3–		

132 +/−

3	**13+**	**3+**	**3−**	
			2−	
3+	**1−**	**9+**		**7+**
		2−	**3−**	
4−				**2**

3−	4−		12+	2−
	10+	3+		
				9+
10+	8+			
		2−		

134 +/−

6+	9+		2−	
	3−	8+	7+	
			1−	9+
1−	3+			
	1−		3−	

+/− **135**

8+		3+	4	4−
4	3+		5+	
4+		5		4
	7+		3−	
2	9+		2−	

136 +/−

6+			14+	
1−	1−			4+
	9+	1−		
3+			1−	
	4−		7+	

1−		6+	2−	
4	6+		3	3+
2−		1−		
	1−	1	3−	
2		6+		4

138 +/−

10+			1−	4−
7+				
12+	6+			1−
	9+	4+		
			3−	

+/− **139**

4−		8+	2	3−
5+	3		9+	
	5+			3−
3+		1−		
4	3−		4+	

140 +/−

13+		6+		
	6+			9+
1−	3+	4−		
		9+	1−	1−
4−				

+/− 141

1	8+		5+	9+
6+		3+		
8+			3−	
9+	2	5+		5+
	2−		5	

142 +/−

1−		6+		
1−		4−		2−
6+	13+		2−	
	1−			4−
		7+		

+/– **143**

1–		**8**+		**4**
5	**7**+		**1**	**1**–
4+	**9**+		**2**–	
	1–	**1**		**4**–
4		**3**–		

144 +/−

1−		**13+**		**9+**
4+	**8+**		**2−**	
1−		**1−**	**3+**	
7+			**4−**	

1−	4−		1−	12+
	6+	6+		
			10+	
6+				
2−		7+		

146 +/−

8+			3−	
4−	1−	5+		6+
		7+		
7+	10+			
		10+		

6+			**8+**	**1−**
8+	**9+**			
	13+			**7+**
1−		**8+**		

148 +/−

1−		4−		7+
14+	6+		1−	
2−	6+	9+		2−
		1−		

+/− 149

11+				2−
2−	4−		4+	
	1−	9+		4−
2−				
	10+			

150 +/−

8+	**9+**		**1−**	
	6+	**2−**	**7+**	
2−			**2−**	**7+**
	4+	**3−**		
1			**9+**	

2	8+	3–		5
7+		1	5+	
	6+	7+		3–
4–		3	9+	
	3+			3

152 +/−

9+		1−	4−	3
3−	3			2−
	8+		2	
1−	2	9+		1
	3−		8+	

+/− **153**

13+	5+		4−	
		4+		1−
6+		2−		
1−	3+		9+	
	6+		1−	

154 +/−

4−	3+	6+		3
		7+	9+	
2−	3		2−	5
	9+	1		1−
3		7+		

13+		7+		
7+		10+	3−	4+
	2−		8+	
2−		11+		

156 +/−

1−		**7**+		**5**
4	**8**+	**4**+	**7**+	
2−			**2**	**3**−
	2	**9**+		
9+		**1**−		**3**

4+		2−		4
	5	1−	5+	
9+			3−	7+
3	3+			
1−		2	4−	

158 +/−

6+		7+	2	5+
5	1−		6+	
7+		2		6+
	2	4−	4	
1−			1−	

6+	3−	11+		
		11+	6+	1−
2−		12+		3+
2−				

160 +/−

9+			7+	
12+	9+			9+
	3+	4+		
		3−		
6+			1−	

7+	**4**−	**3**−		**3**
		4	**3**+	
3−	**6**+	**8**+		**3**−
		1−	**3**	
2−			**9**+	

162 +/−

1−		7+		2−
7+	11+		4−	
		5+		7+
3−			2−	
	8+			

2	6+		1−	
4−		8+	2−	7+
12+	2−			
			1−	
	1−			5

164 +/−

2−		3−		6+
3−	2−	7+		
			4−	
6+	5+		1−	
		10+		

1−		12+	3−	
1−	4−		8+	
			7+	
9+		6+		
1−			3−	

166 +/−

4−		9+	2	1−
6+			12+	
	10+			6+
	12+			
		1−		

9+		8+		10+
1−	6+			
			12+	
1−	4−			
	9+		1−	

168 ×

1	15×		8×	
15×	8×	10×		12×
			15×	
8×				
12×		10×		

300×				30×
	12×		32×	
6×	1200×			

170 ×

32×		30×		
		15×		12×
90×	40×			
	40×			

× **171**

10×		20×	6×	
6×			20×	60×
	12×			
		4×		
60×				

172 ×/÷

6×		1	20×	
20×	1	12×		2÷
	15×		2÷	
12×		2		15×
1	10×		4	

80×		2÷	15×	
15×				2÷
		45×	2÷	
2÷				15×
	2÷			

174 ×/÷

2	60×	10×	1	12×
15×	2÷	20×		15×
		2÷		
	1	24×		

2	15×	4÷		3
5×		8×		2÷
	4	3÷	5	
8×			15×	
3×		5	2÷	

176 ×/÷

40×			12×	
2÷	12×	10×		
			15×	
60×	15×			2÷
		2÷		

15×			80×	6×
2÷				
2÷	15×	20×		
		4×	15×	
12×				

178 ×/÷

12×			40×	
15×	30×			2÷
		15×		
	8×	2÷		15×

15×	20×		2÷	
		2÷	36×	
20×				2÷
2÷		15×		
6×		20×		

180 ×/÷

12×	15×	2÷		2÷
		75×		
10×			2÷	
		4×		45×
2÷				

×/÷ **181**

15×	2÷		3×	
	20×	2÷		60×
2÷				
	6×			40×
15×				

182 ×/÷

6×	2÷		100×	12×
20×	12×		2÷	
	15×	2÷		30×

12×			40×	
2	15×			
20×	2÷		15×	
	6×	4÷		2÷
		15×		

184 ×/÷

18×		100×		2÷
20×		15×		
			2÷	12×
	2÷			
2÷		60×		

5	4÷		15×	2÷
6×		1		
3÷	2÷	20×		3
		2	2×	5÷
4	15×			

186 ×/÷

15×	10×			2÷
		12×		
2÷		60×		15×
80×			2÷	
	6×			

12×		10×		
	100×	4	18×	2÷
6×		5÷	20×	12×
2÷				

188 ×/÷

60×			15×	2÷
2÷	10×			
		2÷	12×	
3×			2÷	15×
	20×			

2	5×	12×		
12×		10×		20×
	6×		2÷	
5	12×			
4÷		15×		2

190 ×/÷

6×	5	2×	12×	
	4×		15×	4
1		15×		10×
2÷			1	
15×		4	2÷	

×/÷ **191**

4	6×			15×
10×	4÷		20×	
	15×			2
	2÷	10×	3÷	
3			4÷	

192 ×/÷

8×		1	15×	
3	4÷	10×		8×
2÷		3	5×	
	5	2÷		3÷
15×			4	

×/÷ **193**

20×	12×	5×		2
		1	6×	
2÷	10×		12×	4
	2÷	3		5÷
3		20×		

194 ×/÷

5×	12×		10×	
	6×			2÷
	2÷	20×		
2÷			15×	
	60×			

6×	2÷	20×		3
		15×	1	2÷
4×	5		8×	
	3÷			5
5	8×		3×	

196 ×/÷

12×		10×		1
1	20×		2÷	6×
20×		3		
3	2÷		4	20×
2÷		15×		

2÷		15×		
15×		24×	2÷	
			40×	15×
20×				
	2÷		12×	

198 ×/÷

2÷		2÷	5	24×
15×			4×	
3÷	5÷			
	20×	12×	10×	
2			3÷	

6×	15×		1	20×
	1	2÷		
4×	8×		15×	
	6×	5	3÷	
5		4÷		2

200 ×/÷

60×			2÷	
1	2÷	15×		12×
40×		2÷		
	15×	12×		10×
			1	

3	20×			2÷
20×	2÷	3	5×	
		40×		15×
3×			6×	
2÷				1

202 ×/÷

2÷		15×		
6×	2÷		75×	2÷
	20×			
			12×	
15×		2÷		

$\times/\div$ **203**

2×		60×		
	10×	15×	2÷	
3			20×	2÷
80×	3÷			
		6×		

204 ×/÷

8×		3	4÷	15×
5	6×	2÷		
4×			5	2÷
	5÷		6×	
15×		4		1

×/÷ **205**

2÷	15×	4÷		10×
		6×		
3÷	24×	5		
			240×	
10×				

206 +/−/×/÷

4	3−		12×	3+
2−		1		
6×	8+		2÷	4
	1	2÷		15×
3−			5	

7+	**2÷**		**2−**	**9+**
	5+			
15×		**2−**		
3−	**2−**		**80×**	
	8+			

208 +/−/×/÷

7+		4−	12×	3
1	2÷			10×
7+		5+	1	
	1		20×	
15×		4	2÷	

5+		1−		10×
2÷	12+			
	20×	4−	4+	
15×			8×	
	5+		3−	

210 +/−/×/÷

20×	**3**	**2÷**		**4−**
	8×	**7+**	**3**	
3			**5+**	
6+		**3**	**9+**	**6×**
2	**3−**			

13+		8×		
	2÷		12×	10+
7+	3−			
		8+		
	120×			

212 +/−/×/÷

12×		2÷	4−	
7+	4+		6×	
		3−		10×
5+	15×		4+	
	7+			4

+/−/×/÷ 213

10×	**2÷**		**1−**	
	1−	**9+**		**6+**
3−		**3**	**2÷**	
	4−			**6×**
7+		**6+**		

214 +/−/×/÷

10+	7+		8+	
		2÷		
	10+			1−
72×		20×		
			2÷	

30×			3−	
9+	10×	12×		3+
		2÷	45×	
2−				
	3−		7+	

216 +/−/×/÷

3−		**10+**		
9+	**30×**	**4+**	**3−**	
			40×	**2÷**
2÷		**15×**		

+/−/×/÷ 217

3−		11+	8+	
6+			30×	
	2÷		3−	
13+		6×		5+

218 +/−/×/÷

3−	2÷	4+		60×
		10+		
3−			2÷	
7+				7+
	10+			

+/−/×/÷ 219

11+		**2÷**	**10×**	
	10×		**45×**	
		12+		
3−	**4+**			**10+**

220 +/−/×/÷

12×	5+	1	10×	
		9+	4−	4
7+	1			4+
	8×		3	
1	15×		2÷	

75×		8+		2÷
	1−			
6×	9+		100×	
10+			1−	

222 +/−/×/÷

17+	6×			8×
2÷	8+	20×		
		1−		2−
2÷		1−		

10×	1−	8+		12+
		3−		
	8×			
9+		1−	2÷	
12×			4−	

224 +/−/×/÷

14+		6×		
		4−	3+	24+
60×				
	2÷			
			2÷	

+/−/×/÷ 225

10+			**1−**	
60×		**2÷**		**15×**
10×		**2−**		
	2÷		**80×**	
6+				

226 +/−/×/÷

13+	6000×			6+
4−	1−		3−	
	1−		4÷	

+/−/×/÷ 227

16+			2÷	
40×		8+		2−
	10+	10×		
			240×	

228 +/−/×/÷

9+			2÷	
2÷		16×	22+	
8+				12×
1−				

15×	6+		11+	
		1−		
	2÷		45×	
11+		2÷		
	60×			

230 +/−/×/÷

9+			**4−**	
9+	**2÷**		**4+**	**40×**
	60×			
		2÷		
3−		**10+**		

4−		18×		9+
2÷	2÷			
	60×	10+		
		2÷	2−	
1−			7+	

232 +/−/×/÷

4	4+	15×		2÷
2÷		7+		
	3−		12×	4−
8+		2		
10×		5+		3

9+		180×	2÷	2−
2÷	4−			
				11+
10+		2÷		
	8+			

234 +/−/×/÷

8+		8×		
7+			100×	1−
6×	3−			
		6×		4−
	12+			

2÷		15×		
3−	4+	8+		2÷
		2÷	1−	
10×				2−
2−		2÷		

236 +/−/×/÷

4−		9+		
240×		6+	4×	
				2−
2÷	12+			
	120×			

12×			16+	
	16+			
12+				9+
		4−		
1−				

238 +/−/×/÷

10+			3−	
24×		4−	8+	
	10+		2÷	
2÷		2−		6×
		5+		

+/−/×/÷ 239

4+	3−		8+	4
	20×	2		2÷
4		4+		
10×	3	3−		15×
	5+		2	

240 +/−/×/÷

6×		**3−**		**28+**
		225×		**8×**
2÷	**6+**			

1−	7+		60×	
		2÷		
6+	1−		2÷	6+
	10+	75×		

242 +/−/×/÷

150×		**12×**		**2÷**
			10+	
8+	**2÷**			**4−**
	9+			
		10+		

+/−/×/÷   243

2÷		**7+**	**36×**	**100×**	
12×	**3÷**				
		11+			**18×**
	8+		**3+**		
20+		**9+**		**5+**	**2÷**
		3−			

244 +/−/×/÷

2÷		18×	5−		5
4−			4	6×	7+
9+	4	15×			
	5−	3÷		5	
10×		1	20×		3−
	7+		3+		

+/−/×/÷ 245

3	40×			6+	18×
11+		7+			
10×			2÷		2
	5−	7+		30×	
3−		54×	7+	9+	
				2÷	

246 +/−/×/÷

9+	5−		12×	2	30×
	5+			7+	
18×			5		3−
6+	6	8+			
	1−	24×			3
		2÷		10×	

248 +/−/×/÷

10+	7+	36×			4
		11+		3÷	
	2−		10+		13+
1−	72×			2÷	
	4−		5+		
6	2÷			2−	

2÷		3+	9+		1
10×			5+	3	18×
2÷	20×	4		30×	
		9+	6		7+
3−			1−	2÷	
3	11+				4

+/−/×/÷ 249

9+	**20×**		**5−**		**3**
	1−		**30×**	**7+**	
	2÷	**3−**		**4**	**3−**
3			**2÷**		
24×			**3**	**24×**	**11+**
7+		**1**			

250 +/−/×/÷

3÷		**8+**	**5+**	**15+**	
8×					
	3−		**13+**		
2−		**96×**	**3÷**		**6+**
11+	**12×**			**12×**	
		4−			

ANSWERS

1

3 3	3 1	2
6 1	2	3
5 2	3	1 1

2

3 2	4 1	3
1	5 3	3 2
3 3	2	1

3

5 3	3 1	2
2	3 3	4 1
3 1	2	3

4

3 2	5 3	1 1
1	2	5 3
4 3	1	2

5

1– 2	4+ 3	1
3	1 1	5+ 2
3+ 1	2	3

6

3 3	1– 2	1
3+ 2	1	5+ 3
2– 1	3	2

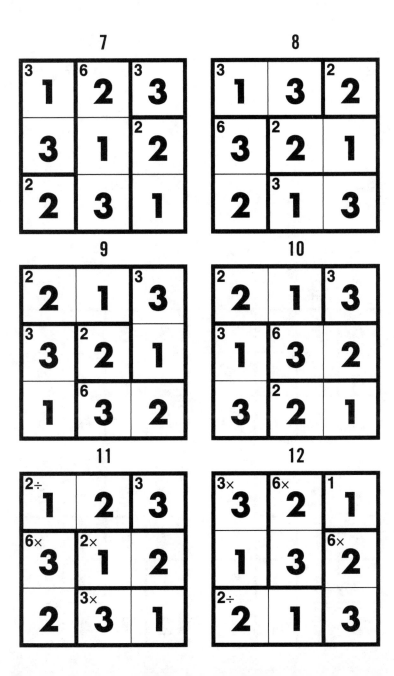

13

2 **2**	3÷ **1**	**3**
4+ **1**	**3**	1− **2**
6× **3**	**2**	**1**

14

5+ **3**	**2**	2− **1**
2÷ **2**	**1**	**3**
1 **1**	6× **3**	**2**

15

4 **1**	**3**	6 **4**	**2**
7 **4**	3 **2**	4 **3**	**1**
3	**1**	3 **2**	7 **4**
6 **2**	**4**	**1**	**3**

16

1 **1**	7 **4**	**3**	3 **2**
7 **4**	3 **3**	3 **2**	**1**
3	3 **2**	**1**	7 **4**
2 **2**	**1**	4 **4**	**3**

17

5 **1**	5 **2**	**3**	4 **4**
4	5 **1**	5 **2**	**3**
3 **3**	**4**	5 **1**	3 **2**
5 **2**	**3**	**4**	**1**

18

7 **3**	2 **2**	3 **1**	4 **4**
4	7 **3**	**2**	3 **1**
3 **1**	**4**	3 **3**	**2**
2	5 **1**	**4**	3 **3**

19

3	2	1	4
2	1	4	3
1	4	3	2
4	3	2	1

20

1	3	4	2
4	2	3	1
3	1	2	4
2	4	1	3

21

3	4	1	2
2	3	4	1
1	2	3	4
4	1	2	3

22

1	2	3	4
3	4	1	2
4	1	2	3
2	3	4	1

23

1	4	3	2
4	3	2	1
3	2	1	4
2	1	4	3

24

1	4	3	2
2	1	4	3
3	2	1	4
4	3	2	1

25

⁵2	3	⁵4	1
⁸4	³1	2	⁷3
1	⁵2	3	4
3	⁷4	1	2

26

⁴1	⁷4	3	⁶2
3	³2	1	4
⁶4	⁴3	³2	1
2	1	⁷4	3

27

⁷1	2	³3	⁷4
4	⁵1	³2	3
³3	4	1	⁷2
⁵2	3	4	1

28

⁶2	⁷3	4	⁶1
4	⁴1	2	3
1	2	⁴3	⁶4
⁷3	4	1	2

29

³3	⁷4	⁷2	1
⁷2	3	¹1	4
1	⁶2	4	⁵3
4	⁴1	3	2

30

³3	⁵4	³1	2
⁵4	1	²2	⁷3
1	²2	⁷3	4
⁵2	3	4	¹1

31

⁹4	⁶3	2	1
3	³2	⁵1	4
2	1	⁹4	3
⁸1	4	3	2

32

³2	⁷4	⁴1	3
1	3	⁷4	³2
⁶4	2	3	1
⁴3	1	⁶2	4

33

³3	⁷4	⁸1	³2
³2	3	4	1
1	²2	3	⁷4
⁷4	1	2	3

34

⁸1	⁹3	4	2
4	³2	⁴3	1
3	1	³2	⁷4
⁶2	4	1	3

35

⁶4	2	⁷3	³1
³1	⁷3	4	2
2	4	⁴1	3
⁴3	1	⁶2	4

36

⁷2	1	4	⁵3
⁵1	4	⁶3	2
⁷4	⁵3	2	1
3	2	⁵1	4

37

³3	³2	1	⁷4
³2	¹1	⁷4	3
1	⁷4	3	²2
⁴4	3	³2	1

38

⁷2	⁸3	4	1
1	⁵2	3	⁹4
4	⁸1	³2	3
3	4	1	2

39

⁵1	⁵3	2	⁴4
4	³2	⁴1	3
⁵3	1	⁴4	³2
2	⁷4	3	1

40

3+ 1	7+ 3	4	1- 2
2	3- 4	1	3
9+ 4	2	2- 3	1
3	7+ 1	2	4

41

³3	1- 2	1	7+ 4
3+ 2	9+ 1	4	3
1	4	5+ 3	2
⁴4	1- 3	2	¹1

42

3- 4	5+ 2	4+ 3	1
1	3	2- 4	2
2- 3	1	1- 2	7+ 4
6+ 2	4	1	3

43

2− 3	3+ 1	2	7+ 4
1	1− 3	7+ 4	2
6+ 4	2	3	1
2	3− 4	1	3 3

44

1− 4	2− 3	1	7+ 2
3	9+ 2	4	1
8+ 2	1	3	4
1	4	5+ 2	3

45

5+ 3	2	3− 1	4
3+ 2	5+ 1	4	1− 3
1	1− 4	3	2
7+ 4	3	1− 2	1

46

1 1	7+ 4	3 3	3+ 2
1− 4	3	1− 2	1
3	3+ 2	1	4 4
2 2	1	7+ 4	3

47

6+ 3	9+ 4	1− 1	2
1	2	7+ 3	4
2	3	2− 4	4+ 1
3− 4	1	2	3

48

7+ 3	3− 4	1	5+ 2
4	3+ 1	1− 2	3
3+ 1	2	3	5+ 4
2	7+ 3	4	1

49

6+ 1	3	2	4 **4**
7+ 4	7+ 2	2− 1	3
3	1	4	3+ 2
2 **2**	1− 4	3	1

50

6+ 1	11+ 3	4	1− 2
2	4	4+ 1	3
3	1	2	8+ 4
2− 4	2	3	1

51

8+ 3	4	1	7+ 2
7+ 2	3	7+ 4	1
6+ 1	2	3	4
4	1	1− 2	3

52

1− 1	2	11+ 4	3
9+ 2	2− 3	1	4
3	3− 4	3+ 2	1
4	1	1− 3	2

53

1− 2	8+ 1	4	3
1	9+ 4	3	1− 2
12+ 4	3	2	1
3	2	3− 1	4

54

2 **2**	12 **3**	4	3 **1**
4 **4**	1 **1**	6 **2**	3
1	8 **2**	3	4 **4**
3 **3**	4	2 **1**	2

55

¹1	¹²3	4	²2
¹²4	²2	⁶3	1
3	⁴1	2	¹²4
²2	4	¹1	3

56

¹²4	⁶3	2	1
1	¹²4	3	²⁴2
3	⁴2	⁴1	4
2	1	4	3

57

⁴4	²2	²1	³3
1	¹²3	2	⁴4
⁶2	4	³3	1
3	⁴1	4	²2

58

⁸2	⁴4	³3	1
4	²2	⁴1	⁶3
³3	1	4	2
1	⁶3	2	⁴4

59

¹²3	⁴1	4	⁶2
4	⁶2	²1	3
²1	3	2	⁴4
2	¹²4	3	1

60

⁸2	¹²3	4	¹1
4	⁴1	⁶2	3
³3	4	¹1	⁸2
1	⁶2	3	4

61

⁴1	¹²4	3	²2
4	⁶3	2	1
²2	1	⁴4	¹²3
⁶3	2	1	4

62

⁶3	⁴1	4	²2
2	¹²4	³3	1
¹1	3	²2	¹²4
⁸4	2	1	3

63

⁶3	⁸2	4	⁴1
2	⁴1	³3	4
⁴1	4	⁶2	3
4	³3	²1	2

64

²⁴4	2	3	⁶1
²1	³3	⁴4	2
2	⁴4	1	3
³3	1	⁸2	4

65

³3	²2	⁴1	4
²2	1	⁴4	⁶3
1	⁴4	⁶3	2
¹²4	3	2	¹1

66

⁶2	3	¹1	¹²4
1	²2	¹²4	3
⁴4	1	3	⁴2
¹²3	4	2	1

67

¹1	³3	⁸4	2
⁶3	1	²2	¹²4
2	⁴4	1	3
⁸4	2	³3	1

68

¹1	4	¹⁸3	2
²⁴2	1	⁴4	3
4	⁶3	2	⁴1
3	²2	1	4

69

¹²3	4	⁴1	²2
⁶2	3	4	1
⁴1	²2	¹²3	4
4	1	⁶2	3

70

³1	3	⁴4	⁸2
³3	⁴1	²2	4
⁸2	4	1	³3
4	²2	³3	1

71

⁶2	3	⁴4	1
⁴4	1	⁶2	¹²3
³1	⁸2	3	4
3	4	²1	2

72

⁶3	2	1	⁴4
¹²4	3	¹²2	1
²1	⁴4	3	2
2	1	¹²4	3

73

2 [8]	1 [12]	4	3
4	3 [12]	2 [6]	1 [8]
1 [3]	4	3	2
3	2 [2]	1	4

74

4 [4]	1 [2]	3 [12]	2 [6]
1 [2]	2	4	3
2	3 [3]	1	4 [4]
3 [24]	4	2	1

75

2 [2]	1	4 [12]	3
1	4 [4]	3 [6]	2
4 [24]	3 [6]	2	1 [1]
3	2	1 [4]	4

76

3 [9]	1 [2]	2	4 [32]
1	3	4	2
4 [8]	2 [6]	3	1 [3]
2	4 [4]	1	3

77

2 [6]	3	4 [4]	1
3 [12]	4 [4]	1	2 [6]
4	1 [2]	2	3
1	2 [24]	3	4

78

2 [6]	1 [12]	4	3
3	2 [8]	1 [4]	4
1	4	3 [6]	2
4 [24]	3	2	1

79

2÷ 2	4	12× 3	1 1
12× 3	1 1	4	6× 2
4	2÷ 2	1	3
1 1	6× 3	2	4 4

80

2÷ 1	2÷ 4	2	12× 3
2	12× 1	3	4
72× 3	2	4	1
4	3	2÷ 1	2

81

3 3	16× 1	4	2÷ 2
2÷ 2	4	3 3	1
1	6× 3	2	12× 4
8× 4	2	1	3

82

2÷ 1	48× 4	3	6× 2
2	6× 1	4	3
24× 4	3	2	4× 1
3	2	1	4

83

2÷ 1	24× 2	3	4
2	12× 3	4× 4	1
12× 3	4	1	6× 2
4	2÷ 1	2	3

84

12× 4	1	24× 3	2
6× 2	3	2× 1	4
3	2÷ 4	2	1
1	2	12× 4	3

85

8× 2	4	12× 1	3
3× 1	3	4	8× 2
12× 3	1	12× 2	4
4	2	3	1

86

12× 3	2÷ 2	1	2÷ 4
1	12× 4	3	2
4	3 3	2÷ 2	1
2÷ 2	1	12× 4	3

87

1 1	12× 4	6× 3	2
2÷ 4	3	2÷ 2	1
2	2÷ 1	4 4	12× 3
3 3	2	1	4

88

6× 3	2÷ 2	1	48× 4
2	1	4	3
12× 4	3	2÷ 2	1
1	24× 4	3	2

89

2÷ 2	1	12× 4	3
12× 1	12× 4	3	8× 2
3	6× 2	1	4
4	3	2÷ 2	1

90

8× 4	1	2	12× 3
12× 2	3	12× 4	1
12× 1	2	3	4
3	4	2÷ 1	2

91

2÷ **1**	2÷ **4**	**2**	12× **3**
2	2÷ **1**	12× **3**	**4**
36× **3**	**2**	**4**	2÷ **1**
4	**3**	**1**	**2**

92

2× **2**	**1**	24× **4**	**3**
1	24× **4**	**3**	**2**
36× **3**	**2**	**1**	8× **4**
4	**3**	**2**	**1**

93

7+ **3**	2÷ **2**	**4**	1− **1**
4	4+ **3**	**1**	**2**
2÷ **2**	**1**	6× **3**	1− **4**
3− **1**	**4**	**2**	**3**

94

4+ **3**	**1**	3+ **2**	4 **4**
2 **2**	8× **4**	**1**	3× **3**
4× **4**	**2**	3 **3**	**1**
1	12× **3**	**4**	2 **2**

95

7+ **3**	**4**	6× **2**	1− **1**
3− **4**	**1**	**3**	**2**
2÷ **2**	1− **3**	4÷ **1**	**4**
1	**2**	12× **4**	**3**

96

6× **3**	1 **1**	6+ **2**	**4**
2	8× **4**	1 **1**	3× **3**
4 **4**	**2**	7+ **3**	**1**
4+ **1**	**3**	**4**	2 **2**

97

4+ **3**	2÷ **2**	3− **1**	**4**
1	**4**	7+ **3**	6× **2**
1− **2**	**1**	**4**	**3**
24× **4**	**3**	**2**	**1**

98

6+ **2**	1 **1**	7+ **3**	**4**
4	3× **3**	**1**	2 **2**
4× **1**	**4**	2 **2**	4+ **3**
3 **3**	8× **2**	**4**	**1**

99

2÷ **2**	12× **3**	**4**	**1**
4	3+ **1**	**2**	36× **3**
2− **1**	6+ **2**	**3**	**4**
3	**4**	1− **1**	**2**

100

2 **2**	7+ **4**	**3**	4+ **1**
6+ **4**	**2**	1 **1**	**3**
3× **3**	1 **1**	8× **4**	**2**
1	5+ **3**	**2**	4 **4**

101

5+ **1**	3 **3**	8× **2**	**4**
4	6+ **2**	3× **1**	3 **3**
2 **2**	**4**	**3**	2÷ **1**
2− **3**	**1**	4 **4**	**2**

102

9+ **1**	**4**	6+ **3**	**2**
4	12× **3**	**2**	**1**
6× **3**	**2**	48× **1**	**4**
2	**1**	**4**	**3**

103

4⁴	2³⁺	1	3³
1⁴⁺	3⁶ˣ	2	4⁸ˣ
3	1⁵⁺	4¹²ˣ	2
2²	4	3	1¹

104

2³⁺	3⁷⁺	4	1¹
1	2²÷	3¹⁻	4
3¹²ˣ	4	1¹	2⁶ˣ
4	1²÷	2	3

105

2²	1⁵⁺	4	3³
3¹²ˣ	2²÷	1	4³⁻
4	3⁷⁺	2⁶ˣ	1
1¹	4	3	2²

106

2²÷	3⁷⁺	4	1¹
4	1²÷	2	3⁵⁺
3¹⁻	4	1¹	2
1¹⁻	2	3¹²ˣ	4

107

2²÷	1	4¹⁻	3
1³⁻	4¹⁻	3	2¹⁻
4	3⁵⁺	2	1
3⁵⁺	2	1⁵⁺	4

108

3⁶⁺	2	1	4¹²ˣ
2⁸ˣ	1³⁻	4⁷⁺	3
1	4	3	2²÷
4	3⁶ˣ	2	1

109

12× 4	3÷ 1	3	2× 2
3	1− 4	2÷ 2	1
1− 2	3	1	7+ 4
1	6+ 2	4	3

110

4+ 3	1	2÷ 2	12× 4
6+ 2	4	1	3
3− 4	6× 2	2− 3	1
1	3	2÷ 4	2

111

2× 1	12× 4	3	2 2
2	1 1	7+ 4	3
12× 4	6× 3	2	1 1
3	2 2	5+ 1	4

112

1− 2	3	5+ 1	4
2÷ 1	2	12× 4	3
7+ 3	2÷ 4	2	1− 1
4	4+ 1	3	2

113

8+ 1	24× 4	3	2
4	7+ 3	2	12× 1
3	2	3− 1	4
2÷ 2	1	4	3

114

3− 4	1	5+ 3	2
3÷ 1	2 2	12× 4	3
3	2÷ 4	2	5+ 1
2 2	2− 3	1	4

115

3−**1**	**4**	5+**3**	**2**
9+**4**	**3**	**2**	12×**1**
6×**3**	2÷**2**	**1**	**4**
2	5+**1**	**4**	**3**

116

2**2**	12×**3**	**4**	2÷**1**
7+**3**	**4**	1**1**	**2**
5+**1**	2**2**	1−**3**	**4**
4	3+**1**	**2**	3**3**

117

7+**2**	**1**	**4**	9+**3**
5+**1**	**4**	2−**3**	**2**
12×**3**	1−**2**	**1**	**4**
4	**3**	2÷**2**	**1**

118

2**2**	7+**4**	**3**	3÷**1**
12×**4**	3+**2**	**1**	**3**
3	4÷**1**	**4**	2**2**
4+**1**	**3**	8×**2**	**4**

119

2÷**2**	**1**	48×**4**	**3**
4+**3**	1−**2**	**1**	**4**
1	7+**4**	**3**	5+**2**
12×**4**	**3**	**2**	**1**

120

18×**2**	**3**	16×**4**	1−**1**
3	**4**	**1**	**2**
5+**4**	2÷**1**	5+**2**	**3**
1	**2**	1−**3**	**4**

121

7+ 4	3	2÷ 1	2
3+ 1	2÷ 4	2	12× 3
2	2- 1	3	4
1- 3	2	5+ 4	1

122

3- 4	1	72× 2	3
2÷ 1	9+ 2	3	4
2	3	4	1- 1
8+ 3	4	1	2

123

2- 3	5+ 4	1	2÷ 2
1	72× 2	3	4
8× 2	3	4	6+ 1
4	1	2	3

124

5+ 3	1- 2	1	12× 4
2	3- 1	7+ 4	3
4÷ 1	4	3	2÷ 2
4	6× 3	2	1

125

96× 4	2÷ 1	2	1- 3
3	4	6+ 1	2
2	6× 3	4	1
1	2	1- 3	4

126

5+ 1	3 3	2÷ 4	2
4	6× 2	3	1 1
4+ 3	1	2 2	12× 4
2 2	3- 4	1	3

127

4 **4**	12× **2**	2− **1**	**3**
2÷ **1**	**3**	**2**	3− **4**
2	11+ **4**	**3**	**1**
4+ **3**	**1**	**4**	2 **2**

128

7+ **2**	**1**	**4**	2− **3**
12× **4**	**3**	2 **2**	**1**
1	4 **4**	24× **3**	**2**
6× **3**	**2**	**1**	**4**

129

1− **3**	**2**	9+ **5**	**4**	1 **1**
2 **2**	4− **1**	7+ **4**	**3**	1− **5**
6+ **1**	**5**	3 **3**	1− **2**	**4**
5	4 **4**	3+ **2**	**1**	5+ **3**
7+ **4**	**3**	**1**	5 **5**	**2**

130

1 **1**	2− **4**	**2**	10+ **3**	**5**
1− **3**	6+ **1**	14+ **4**	**5**	**2**
4	**2**	**5**	2− **1**	**3**
3− **5**	**3**	1− **1**	**2**	9+ **4**
2	2− **5**	**3**	**4**	**1**

131

1− **2**	4+ **3**	**1**	1− **4**	5 **5**
1	7+ **2**	**5**	**3**	1− **4**
9+ **5**	3− **1**	**4**	2 **2**	**3**
4	9+ **5**	4+ **3**	**1**	3+ **2**
3 **3**	**4**	3− **2**	**5**	**1**

132

3 **3**	13+ **4**	3+ **1**	3− **2**	**5**
4	**5**	**2**	2− **3**	**1**
3+ **1**	1− **2**	9+ **4**	**5**	7+ **3**
2	**3**	2− **5**	3− **1**	**4**
4− **5**	**1**	**3**	**4**	2 **2**

133

³⁻4	⁴⁻1	5	¹²⁺3	²⁻2
1	¹⁰⁺3	³⁺2	5	4
5	2	1	4	⁹⁺3
¹⁰⁺2	⁸⁺4	3	1	5
3	5	²⁻4	2	1

134

⁶⁺2	⁹⁺5	4	²⁻1	3
1	³⁻4	⁸⁺3	⁷⁺5	2
3	1	5	¹⁻2	⁹⁺4
¹⁻4	³⁺2	1	3	5
5	¹⁻3	2	³⁻4	1

135

⁸⁺5	3	³⁺2	⁴4	⁴⁻1
⁴4	³⁺2	1	⁵⁺3	5
⁴⁺3	1	⁵5	2	⁴4
1	⁷⁺4	3	³⁻5	2
²2	⁹⁺5	4	²⁻1	3

136

⁶⁺3	2	1	¹⁴⁺4	5
¹⁻4	¹⁻3	2	5	⁴⁺1
5	⁹⁺4	¹⁻3	1	2
³⁺1	5	4	¹⁻2	3
2	⁴⁻1	5	⁷⁺3	4

137

¹⁻1	2	⁶⁺4	²⁻5	3
⁴4	⁶⁺5	2	³3	³⁺1
²⁻5	1	¹⁻3	4	2
3	¹⁻4	¹1	³⁻2	5
²2	3	⁶⁺5	1	⁴4

138

¹⁰⁺2	3	5	¹⁻4	⁴⁻1
⁷⁺1	2	4	3	5
¹²⁺5	⁶⁺1	3	2	¹⁻4
4	⁹⁺5	⁴⁺2	1	3
3	4	1	³⁻5	2

139

⁴⁻ 5	1	⁸⁺ 3	² 2	³⁻ 4
⁵⁺ 2	³ 3	5	⁹⁺ 4	1
3	⁵⁺ 4	1	5	³⁻ 2
³⁺ 1	2	¹⁻ 4	3	5
⁴ 4	³⁻ 5	2	⁴⁺ 1	3

140

¹³⁺ 5	4	⁶⁺ 3	2	1
4	⁶⁺ 3	2	1	⁹⁺ 5
¹⁻ 3	³⁺ 2	⁴⁻ 1	5	4
2	1	⁹⁺ 5	¹⁻ 4	¹⁻ 3
⁴⁻ 1	5	4	3	2

141

¹ 1	⁸⁺ 3	5	⁵⁺ 2	⁹⁺ 4
⁶⁺ 2	4	³⁺ 1	3	5
⁸⁺ 3	5	2	³⁻ 4	1
⁹⁺ 5	² 2	⁵⁺ 4	1	⁵⁺ 3
4	²⁻ 1	3	⁵ 5	2

142

¹⁻ 5	4	⁶⁺ 2	1	3
¹⁻ 4	3	⁴⁻ 1	5	²⁻ 2
⁶⁺ 1	¹³⁺ 5	3	²⁻ 2	4
3	¹⁻ 2	5	4	⁴⁻ 1
2	1	⁷⁺ 4	3	5

143

¹⁻ 2	1	⁸⁺ 5	3	⁴ 4
⁵ 5	⁷⁺ 4	3	¹ 1	¹⁻ 2
⁴⁺ 1	⁹⁺ 5	4	²⁻ 2	3
3	¹⁻ 2	¹ 1	4	⁴⁻ 5
⁴ 4	3	³⁻ 2	5	1

144

¹⁻ 2	1	¹³⁺ 5	4	⁹⁺ 3
⁴⁺ 1	⁸⁺ 5	4	²⁻ 3	2
3	2	1	5	4
¹⁻ 5	4	¹⁻ 3	³⁺ 2	1
⁷⁺ 4	3	2	⁴⁻ 1	5

145

4 (1−)	1 (4−)	5	2 (1−)	3 (12+)
5	2 (6+)	1 (6+)	3	4
1	3	2	4 (10+)	5
2 (6+)	4	3	5	1
3 (2−)	5	4 (7+)	1	2

146

4 (8+)	3	1	2 (3−)	5
5 (4−)	4 (1−)	2 (5+)	3	1 (6+)
1	5	3 (7+)	4	2
2 (7+)	1 (10+)	4	5	3
3	2	5 (10+)	1	4

147

3 (6+)	2	1	4 (8+)	5 (1−)
2 (8+)	1 (9+)	5	3	4
5	4 (13+)	3	1	2 (7+)
1	5	4	2	3
4 (1−)	3	2 (8+)	5	1

148

2 (1−)	3	5 (4−)	1	4 (7+)
5 (14+)	1 (6+)	3	4 (1−)	2
4	5	2	3	1
1 (2−)	2 (6+)	4 (9+)	5	3 (2−)
3	4	1 (1−)	2	5

149

1 (11+)	3	2	5	4 (2−)
4 (2−)	1 (4−)	5	3 (4+)	2
2	4 (1−)	3 (9+)	1	5 (4−)
3 (2−)	5	4	2	1
5	2 (10+)	1	4	3

150

3 (8+)	5 (9+)	4	2 (1−)	1
5	2 (6+)	1 (2−)	4 (7+)	3
2 (2−)	4	3	1 (2−)	5 (7+)
4	1 (4+)	5 (3−)	3	2
1 (1)	3	2 (9+)	5	4

151

^{2}2	$^{8+}$3	$^{3-}$4	1	^{5}5
$^{7+}$4	5	^{1}1	$^{5+}$3	2
3	$^{6+}$4	$^{7+}$5	2	$^{3-}$1
$^{4-}$1	2	^{3}3	$^{9+}$5	4
5	$^{3+}$1	2	4	^{3}3

152

$^{9+}$5	4	$^{1-}$2	$^{4-}$1	^{3}3
$^{3-}$4	^{3}3	1	5	$^{2-}$2
1	$^{8+}$5	3	^{2}2	4
$^{1-}$3	^{2}2	$^{9+}$5	4	^{1}1
2	$^{3-}$1	4	$^{8+}$3	5

153

$^{13+}$4	$^{5+}$3	2	$^{4-}$5	1
5	4	$^{4+}$3	1	$^{1-}$2
$^{6+}$1	5	$^{2-}$4	2	3
$^{1-}$3	$^{3+}$2	1	$^{9+}$4	5
2	$^{6+}$1	5	$^{1-}$3	4

154

$^{4-}$5	$^{3+}$1	$^{6+}$2	4	^{3}3
1	2	$^{7+}$3	$^{9+}$5	4
$^{2-}$2	^{3}3	4	$^{2-}$1	^{5}5
4	$^{9+}$5	^{1}1	3	$^{1-}$2
^{3}3	4	$^{7+}$5	2	1

155

$^{13+}$5	3	$^{7+}$1	2	4
$^{7+}$2	5	$^{10+}$3	$^{3-}$4	$^{4+}$1
4	2	5	1	3
1	$^{2-}$4	2	$^{8+}$3	5
$^{2-}$3	1	$^{11+}$4	5	2

156

$^{1-}$2	1	$^{7+}$4	3	^{5}5
^{4}4	$^{8+}$3	$^{4+}$1	$^{7+}$5	2
$^{2-}$1	5	3	^{2}2	$^{3-}$4
3	^{2}2	$^{9+}$5	4	1
$^{9+}$5	4	$^{1-}$2	1	^{3}3

157

4+ 2	1	2− 5	3	4 4
1	5 5	1− 4	5+ 2	3
9+ 5	4	3	3− 1	7+ 2
3 3	3+ 2	1	4	5
1− 4	3	2 2	4− 5	1

158

6+ 1	5	7+ 4	2 2	5+ 3
5 5	1− 4	3	6+ 1	2
7+ 4	3	2 2	5	6+ 1
3	2 2	4− 1	4 4	5
1− 2	1	5	1− 3	4

159

6+ 3	3− 1	11+ 2	4	5
1	4	11+ 5	6+ 2	1− 3
2	5	1	3	4
2− 5	3	12+ 4	1	3+ 2
2− 4	2	3	5	1

160

9+ 2	4	3	7+ 5	1
12+ 3	9+ 5	4	1	9+ 2
5	3+ 2	4+ 1	3	4
4	1	3− 5	2	3
6+ 1	3	2	1− 4	5

161

7+ 4	4− 1	3− 5	2	3 3
3	5	4 4	3+ 1	2
3− 2	6+ 4	8+ 3	5	3− 1
5	2	1− 1	3 3	4
2− 1	3	2	9+ 4	5

162

1− 1	2	7+ 4	3	2− 5
7+ 4	11+ 5	2	4− 1	3
3	4	5+ 1	5	7+ 2
3− 5	1	3	2− 2	4
2	8+ 3	5	4	1

163

²2	⁶⁺1	5	¹⁻4	3
⁴⁻1	5	⁸⁺4	²⁻3	⁷⁺2
¹²⁺3	²⁻2	1	5	4
5	4	3	¹⁻2	1
4	¹⁻3	2	1	⁵5

164

²⁻3	5	³⁻4	1	⁶⁺2
³⁻5	²⁻2	⁷⁺1	3	4
2	4	3	⁴⁻5	1
⁶⁺1	⁵⁺3	2	¹⁻4	5
4	1	¹⁰⁺5	2	3

165

¹⁻3	2	¹²⁺5	³⁻1	4
¹⁻2	⁴⁻1	4	⁸⁺5	3
1	5	3	⁷⁺4	2
⁹⁺5	4	⁶⁺2	3	1
¹⁻4	3	1	³⁻2	5

166

⁴⁻5	1	⁹⁺3	²2	¹⁻4
⁶⁺1	2	4	¹²⁺3	5
3	¹⁰⁺4	1	5	⁶⁺2
2	¹²⁺3	5	4	1
4	5	¹⁻2	1	3

167

⁹⁺5	4	⁸⁺3	2	¹⁰⁺1
¹⁻4	⁶⁺3	2	1	5
3	2	1	¹²⁺5	4
¹⁻2	⁴⁻1	5	4	3
1	⁹⁺5	4	¹⁻3	2

168

¹1	¹⁵ˣ5	3	⁸ˣ4	2
¹⁵ˣ3	⁸ˣ2	¹⁰ˣ5	1	¹²ˣ4
5	4	2	¹⁵ˣ3	1
⁸ˣ2	1	4	5	3
¹²ˣ4	3	¹⁰ˣ1	2	5

169

300× 4	5	1	3	**30×** 2
5	**12×** 1	2	**32×** 4	3
2	3	4	1	5
6× 3	**1200×** 4	5	2	1
1	2	3	5	4

170

32× 1	4	**30×** 3	2	5
4	2	**15×** 1	5	**12×** 3
90× 2	**40×** 5	4	3	1
5	3	2	1	4
3	**40×** 1	5	4	2

171

10× 5	1	**20×** 4	**6×** 3	2
6× 1	2	5	**20×** 4	**60×** 3
2	**12×** 3	1	5	4
3	4	**4×** 2	1	5
60× 4	5	3	2	1

172

6× 2	3	**1** 1	**20×** 5	4
20× 5	**1** 1	**12×** 4	3	**2÷** 2
4	**15×** 5	3	**2÷** 2	1
12× 3	4	**2** 2	1	**15×** 5
1 1	**10×** 2	5	**4** 4	3

173

80× 4	5	**2÷** 2	**15×** 1	3
15× 3	4	1	5	**2÷** 2
5	1	**45×** 3	**2÷** 2	4
2÷ 2	3	5	4	**15×** 1
1	**2÷** 2	4	3	5

174

2 2	**60×** 3	**10×** 5	**1** 1	**12×** 4
4	5	2	3	1
15× 1	**2÷** 2	**20×** 4	5	**15×** 3
3	4	**2÷** 1	2	5
5	**1** 1	**24×** 3	4	2

175

2 **2**	15× **5**	4÷ **4**	**1**	3 **3**
5× **5**	**3**	8× **2**	**4**	2÷ **1**
1	4 **4**	3÷ **3**	5 **5**	**2**
8× **4**	**2**	**1**	15× **3**	**5**
3× **3**	**1**	5 **5**	2÷ **2**	**4**

176

40× **5**	**2**	**4**	12× **1**	**3**
2÷ **1**	12× **3**	10× **5**	**2**	**4**
2	**4**	**1**	15× **3**	**5**
60× **4**	15× **1**	**3**	**5**	2÷ **2**
3	**5**	2÷ **2**	**4**	**1**

177

15× **5**	**1**	**3**	80× **4**	6× **2**
2÷ **1**	**2**	**4**	**5**	**3**
2÷ **2**	15× **3**	20× **5**	**1**	**4**
4	**5**	4× **2**	15× **3**	**1**
12× **3**	**4**	**1**	**2**	**5**

178

12× **4**	**3**	**1**	40× **2**	**5**
15× **1**	30× **5**	**3**	**4**	2÷ **2**
3	**2**	15× **5**	**1**	**4**
5	8× **4**	2÷ **2**	**3**	15× **1**
2	**1**	**4**	**5**	**3**

179

15× **3**	20× **4**	**5**	2÷ **2**	**1**
5	**1**	2÷ **2**	36× **4**	**3**
20× **4**	**5**	**1**	**3**	2÷ **2**
2÷ **1**	**2**	15× **3**	**5**	**4**
6× **2**	**3**	20× **4**	**1**	**5**

180

12× **3**	15× **5**	2÷ **2**	**4**	2÷ **1**
4	**1**	75× **3**	**5**	**2**
10× **1**	**3**	**5**	2÷ **2**	**4**
5	**2**	4× **4**	**1**	45× **3**
2÷ **2**	**4**	**1**	**3**	**5**

181

15× 5	2÷ 2	4	3× 3	1
3	20× 5	2÷ 2	1	60× 4
2÷ 2	4	1	5	3
4	6× 1	3	2	40× 5
15× 1	3	5	4	2

182

6× 3	2÷ 2	1	100× 5	12× 4
2	1	5	4	3
20× 5	12× 4	3	2÷ 2	1
4	15× 3	2÷ 2	1	30× 5
1	5	4	3	2

183

12× 3	1	4	40× 2	5
2 2	15× 5	3	1	4
20× 1	2÷ 4	2	15× 5	3
5	6× 3	4÷ 1	4	2÷ 2
4	2	15× 5	3	1

184

18× 3	2	100× 5	4	2÷ 1
20× 4	3	15× 1	5	2
1	5	3	2÷ 2	12× 4
5	2÷ 4	2	1	3
2÷ 2	1	60× 4	3	5

185

5 5	4÷ 1	4	15× 3	2÷ 2
6× 2	3	1 1	5	4
3÷ 1	2÷ 2	20× 5	4	3 3
3	4	2 2	2× 1	5÷ 5
4 4	15× 5	3	2	1

186

15× 3	10× 2	1	5	2÷ 4
1	5	12× 4	3	2
2÷ 2	1	60× 5	4	15× 3
80× 5	4	3	2÷ 2	1
4	6× 3	2	1	5

187

12× 4	3	10× 2	1	5
1	100× 5	4 · 4	18× 3	2÷ 2
5	4	3	2	1
6× 3	2	5÷ 1	20× 5	12× 4
2÷ 2	1	5	4	3

188

60× 5	3	4	15× 1	2÷ 2
2÷ 4	10× 2	3	5	1
2	5	2÷ 1	12× 3	4
3× 3	1	2	2÷ 4	15× 5
1	20× 4	5	2	3

189

2 · 2	5× 5	12× 1	4	3
12× 3	1	10× 2	5	20× 4
4	6× 2	3	2÷ 1	5
5	12× 3	4	2	1
4÷ 1	4	15× 5	3	2 · 2

190

6× 2	5 · 5	2× 1	12× 4	3
3	4× 1	2	15× 5	4 · 4
1 · 1	4	15× 5	3	10× 2
2÷ 4	2	3	1 · 1	5
15× 5	3	4 · 4	2÷ 2	1

191

4 · 4	6× 3	1	2	15× 5
10× 2	4÷ 1	4	20× 5	3
1	15× 5	3	4	2 · 2
5	2÷ 4	10× 2	3÷ 3	1
3 · 3	2	5	4÷ 1	4

192

8× 4	2	1 · 1	15× 3	5
3 · 3	4÷ 1	10× 5	2	8× 4
2÷ 1	4	3 · 3	5× 5	2
2	5 · 5	2÷ 4	1	3÷ 3
15× 5	3	2	4 · 4	1

193

20×**4**	12×**3**	5×**5**	**1**	2**2**
5	**4**	1**1**	6×**2**	**3**
2÷**1**	10×**5**	**2**	12×**3**	4**4**
2	2÷**1**	3**3**	**4**	5÷**5**
3**3**	**2**	20×**4**	**5**	**1**

194

5×**1**	12×**4**	**3**	10×**2**	**5**
5	6×**3**	**2**	**1**	2÷**4**
3	2÷**1**	20×**5**	**4**	**2**
2÷**4**	**2**	**1**	15×**5**	**3**
2	60×**5**	**4**	**3**	**1**

195

6×**2**	2÷**1**	20×**4**	**5**	3**3**
3	**2**	15×**5**	1**1**	2÷**4**
4×**1**	5**5**	**3**	8×**4**	**2**
4	3÷**3**	**1**	**2**	5**5**
5**5**	8×**4**	**2**	3×**3**	**1**

196

12×**4**	**3**	10×**2**	**5**	1**1**
1**1**	20×**5**	**4**	2÷**2**	6×**3**
20×**5**	**4**	3**3**	**1**	**2**
3**3**	2÷**2**	**1**	4**4**	20×**5**
2÷**2**	**1**	15×**5**	**3**	**4**

197

2÷**2**	**4**	15×**3**	**5**	**1**
15×**3**	**5**	24×**4**	2÷**1**	**2**
1	**3**	**2**	40×**4**	15×**5**
20×**4**	**1**	**5**	**2**	**3**
5	2÷**2**	**1**	12×**3**	**4**

198

2÷**4**	**2**	2÷**1**	5**5**	24×**3**
15×**5**	**3**	**2**	4×**1**	**4**
3÷**3**	5÷**1**	**5**	**4**	**2**
1	20×**4**	12×**3**	10×**2**	**5**
2**2**	**5**	**4**	3÷**3**	**1**

199

6× **2**	15× **5**	**3**	¹**1**	20× **4**
3	¹**1**	2÷ **4**	**2**	**5**
4× **1**	8× **4**	**2**	15× **5**	**3**
4	6× **2**	⁵**5**	3÷ **3**	**1**
⁵**5**	**3**	4÷ **1**	**4**	²**2**

200

60× **3**	**4**	**5**	2÷ **2**	**1**
¹**1**	2÷ **2**	15× **3**	**5**	12× **4**
40× **5**	**1**	2÷ **2**	**4**	**3**
4	15× **5**	12× **1**	**3**	10× **2**
2	**3**	**4**	¹**1**	**5**

201

³**3**	20× **5**	**1**	**4**	2÷ **2**
20× **5**	2÷ **2**	³**3**	5× **1**	**4**
4	**1**	40× **2**	**5**	15× **3**
3× **1**	**3**	**4**	6× **2**	**5**
2÷ **2**	**4**	**5**	**3**	¹**1**

202

2÷ **4**	**2**	15× **3**	**1**	**5**
6× **3**	2÷ **1**	**2**	75× **5**	2÷ **4**
1	20× **4**	**5**	**3**	**2**
2	**5**	**1**	12× **4**	**3**
15× **5**	**3**	2÷ **4**	**2**	**1**

203

2× **2**	**1**	60× **4**	**3**	**5**
1	10× **5**	15× **3**	2÷ **2**	**4**
³**3**	**2**	**5**	20× **4**	2÷ **1**
80× **4**	3÷ **3**	**1**	**5**	**2**
5	**4**	6× **2**	**1**	**3**

204

8× **2**	**4**	³**3**	4÷ **1**	15× **5**
⁵**5**	6× **2**	2÷ **1**	**4**	**3**
4× **1**	**3**	**2**	⁵**5**	2÷ **4**
4	5÷ **1**	**5**	6× **3**	**2**
15× **3**	**5**	⁴**4**	**2**	¹**1**

205

2÷ **2**	15× **3**	4÷ **4**	**1**	10× **5**
4	**5**	6× **1**	**3**	**2**
3÷ **3**	24× **4**	5 **5**	**2**	**1**
1	**2**	**3**	240× **5**	**4**
10× **5**	**1**	**2**	**4**	**3**

206

4 **4**	3− **2**	**5**	12× **3**	3+ **1**
2− **5**	**3**	1 **1**	**4**	**2**
6× **2**	8+ **5**	**3**	2÷ **1**	4 **4**
3	1 **1**	2÷ **4**	**2**	15× **5**
3− **1**	**4**	**2**	5 **5**	**3**

207

7+ **5**	2÷ **2**	**4**	2− **1**	9+ **3**
2	5+ **4**	**1**	**3**	**5**
15× **3**	**5**	2− **2**	**4**	**1**
3− **4**	2− **1**	**3**	80× **5**	**2**
1	8+ **3**	**5**	**2**	**4**

208

7+ **2**	**5**	4− **1**	12× **4**	3 **3**
1 **1**	2÷ **4**	**5**	**3**	10× **2**
7+ **4**	**2**	5+ **3**	1 **1**	**5**
3	1 **1**	**2**	20× **5**	**4**
15× **5**	**3**	4 **4**	2÷ **2**	**1**

209

5+ **4**	**1**	1− **2**	**3**	10× **5**
2÷ **1**	12+ **3**	**4**	**5**	**2**
2	20× **4**	4− **5**	4+ **1**	**3**
15× **3**	**5**	**1**	8× **2**	**4**
5	5+ **2**	**3**	3− **4**	**1**

210

20× **4**	3 **3**	2÷ **1**	**2**	4− **5**
5	8× **4**	7+ **2**	3 **3**	**1**
3 **3**	**2**	**5**	5+ **1**	**4**
6+ **1**	**5**	3 **3**	9+ **4**	6× **2**
2 **2**	3− **1**	**4**	**5**	**3**

211

13+ 3	5	**8×** 4	2	1
5	**2÷** 2	1	**12×** 4	**10+** 3
7+ 2	**3−** 4	3	1	5
4	1	**8+** 5	3	2
1	**120×** 3	2	5	4

212

12× 3	4	**2÷** 2	**4−** 5	1
7+ 5	**4+** 1	4	**6×** 2	3
2	3	**3−** 1	4	**10×** 5
5+ 4	**15×** 5	3	**4+** 1	2
1	**7+** 2	5	3	**4** 4

213

10× 5	**2÷** 1	2	**1−** 3	4
2	**1−** 3	**9+** 4	5	**6+** 1
3− 1	2	**3** 3	**2÷** 4	5
4	**4−** 5	1	2	**6×** 3
7+ 3	4	**6+** 5	1	2

214

10+ 4	**7+** 5	1	**8+** 3	2
5	1	**2÷** 2	4	3
1	**10+** 2	3	5	**1−** 4
72× 2	3	**20×** 4	1	5
3	4	5	**2÷** 2	1

215

30× 2	3	5	**3−** 1	4
9+ 5	**10×** 1	**12×** 3	4	**3+** 2
4	5	**2÷** 2	**45×** 3	1
2− 1	2	4	5	3
3	**3−** 4	1	**7+** 2	5

216

3− 4	1	**10+** 2	3	5
9+ 5	**30×** 2	**4+** 3	**3−** 4	1
3	5	1	**40×** 2	**2÷** 4
1	3	4	5	2
2÷ 2	4	**15×** 5	1	3

217

3− 4	1	11+ 2	8+ 3	5
6+ 1	3	4	30× 5	2
2	2÷ 4	5	3− 1	3
13+ 5	2	6× 3	4	5+ 1
3	5	1	2	4

218

3− 5	2÷ 2	4+ 1	3	60× 4
2	4	10+ 3	5	1
3− 4	1	5	2÷ 2	3
7+ 1	3	2	4	7+ 5
3	10+ 5	4	1	2

219

11+ 3	4	2÷ 1	10× 2	5
4	10× 5	2	45× 3	1
1	2	12+ 4	5	3
3− 2	4+ 3	5	1	10+ 4
5	1	3	4	2

220

12× 4	5+ 3	1	10× 2	5
3	2	9+ 5	4− 1	4 4
7+ 2	1 1	4	5	4+ 3
5	8× 4	2	3 3	1
1 1	15× 5	3	2÷ 4	2

221

75× 3	5	8+ 4	1	2÷ 2
5	1− 2	1	3	4
6× 2	9+ 4	3	100× 5	1
1	3	2	4	5
10+ 4	1	5	1− 2	3

222

17+ 5	6× 1	2	3	8× 4
3	4	5	1	2
2÷ 2	8+ 3	20× 4	5	1
4	5	1− 1	2	2− 3
2÷ 1	2	1− 3	4	5

223

10×	1−	8+		12+
1	2	5	3	4
2	3	3− 1	4	5
5	8× 1	4	2	3
9+ 4	5	1− 3	2÷ 1	2
12× 3	4	2	4− 5	1

224

14+		6×		
4	5	2	3	1
2	3	4− 5	3+ 1	24+ 4
60× 3	4	1	2	5
1	2÷ 2	4	5	3
5	1	3	2÷ 4	2

225

10+			1−	
4	1	5	3	2
60× 3	5	2÷ 4	2	15× 1
10× 2	4	2− 3	1	5
5	2÷ 2	1	80× 4	3
6+ 1	3	2	5	4

226

13+	6000×			6+
2	5	4	3	1
3	1	5	4	2
4	2	1	5	3
4− 1	1− 4	3	3− 2	5
5	1− 3	2	4÷ 1	4

227

16+			2÷	
3	5	4	1	2
40× 2	4	8+ 3	5	2− 1
4	10+ 1	10× 5	2	3
5	2	1	240× 3	4
1	3	2	4	5

228

9+			2÷	
5	1	3	2	4
2÷ 1	2	16× 4	22+ 3	5
8+ 3	4	1	5	12× 2
2	3	5	4	1
1− 4	5	2	1	3

229

¹⁵ˣ 3	⁶⁺ 4	1	¹¹⁺ 5	2
5	1	¹⁻ 3	2	4
1	²÷ 2	4	⁴⁵ˣ 3	5
¹¹⁺ 4	5	²÷ 2	1	3
2	⁶⁰ˣ 3	5	4	1

230

⁹⁺ 2	4	3	⁴⁻ 5	1
⁹⁺ 5	²÷ 2	1	⁴⁺ 3	⁴⁰ˣ 4
3	⁶⁰ˣ 5	4	1	2
1	3	²÷ 2	4	5
³⁻ 4	1	¹⁰⁺ 5	2	3

231

⁴⁻ 5	1	¹⁸ˣ 3	2	⁹⁺ 4
²÷ 1	²÷ 2	4	3	5
2	⁶⁰ˣ 3	¹⁰⁺ 5	4	1
4	5	²÷ 2	²⁻ 1	3
¹⁻ 3	4	1	⁷⁺ 5	2

232

⁴ 4	⁴⁺ 1	¹⁵ˣ 3	5	²÷ 2
²÷ 1	3	⁷⁺ 5	2	4
2	³⁻ 4	1	¹²ˣ 3	⁴⁻ 5
⁸⁺ 3	5	² 2	4	1
¹⁰ˣ 5	2	⁵⁺ 4	1	³ 3

233

⁹⁺ 5	4	¹⁸⁰ˣ 3	²÷ 2	²⁻ 1
²÷ 2	⁴⁻ 1	5	4	3
1	5	4	3	¹¹⁺ 2
¹⁰⁺ 4	3	²÷ 2	1	5
3	⁸⁺ 2	1	5	4

234

⁸⁺ 5	3	⁸ˣ 2	1	4
⁷⁺ 4	2	1	¹⁰⁰ˣ 5	¹⁻ 3
⁶ˣ 3	³⁻ 1	5	4	2
1	4	⁶ˣ 3	2	⁴⁻ 5
2	¹²⁺ 5	4	3	1

235

2÷ 2	4	**15×** 3	1	5
3− 4	**4+** 1	**8+** 5	3	**2÷** 2
1	3	**2÷** 2	**1−** 5	4
10× 5	2	1	4	**2−** 3
2− 3	5	**2÷** 4	2	1

236

4− 5	1	**9+** 2	3	4
240× 3	4	**6+** 5	**4×** 1	2
4	5	1	2	**2−** 3
2÷ 2	**12+** 3	4	5	1
1	**120×** 2	3	4	5

237

12× 2	1	3	**16+** 4	5
1	**16+** 5	2	3	4
12+ 3	2	4	5	**9+** 1
5	4	**4−** 1	2	3
1− 4	3	5	1	2

238

10+ 5	3	2	**3−** 4	1
24× 4	2	**4−** 1	**8+** 3	5
3	**10+** 1	5	**2÷** 2	4
2÷ 1	4	**2−** 3	5	**6×** 2
2	5	**5+** 4	1	3

239

4+ 1	**3−** 2	5	**8+** 3	**4** 4
3	**20×** 4	**2** 2	5	**2÷** 1
4 4	5	**4+** 3	1	2
10× 2	**3** 3	**3−** 1	4	**15×** 5
5	**5+** 1	4	**2** 2	3

240

6× 3	2	**3−** 1	4	**28+** 5
1	5	4	2	3
5	4	**225×** 3	1	**8×** 2
2÷ 2	**6+** 1	5	3	4
4	3	2	5	1

241

1− 2	7+ 5	1	60× 3	4
3	1	2÷ 2	4	5
6+ 5	1− 3	4	2÷ 1	6+ 2
1	10+ 4	75× 5	2	3
4	2	3	5	1

242

150× 2	5	12× 1	3	2÷ 4
5	3	4	10+ 1	2
8+ 3	2÷ 1	2	4	4− 5
4	9+ 2	3	5	1
1	4	10+ 5	2	3

243

2÷ 2	1	7+ 3	36× 6	100× 5	4
12× 3	3÷ 2	4	1	6	5
1	6	11+ 2	5	4	18× 3
4	8+ 3	5	3+ 2	1	6
20+ 5	4	9+ 6	3	5+ 2	2÷ 1
6	5	3− 1	4	3	2

244

2÷ 4	2	18× 3	5− 1	6	5 5
4− 1	5	6	4 4	6× 3	7+ 2
9+ 6	4 4	15× 5	3	2	1
3	5− 1	3÷ 2	6	5 5	4
10× 2	6	1 1	20× 5	4	3− 3
5	7+ 3	4	3+ 2	1	6

245

3 3	40× 2	5	4	6+ 1	18× 6
11+ 6	5	7+ 2	1	4	3
10× 5	4	1	2÷ 6	3	2 2
2	5− 1	7+ 4	3	30× 6	5
3− 1	6	54× 3	7+ 2	9+ 5	4
4	3	6	5	2÷ 2	1

246

9+ 4	5− 1	6	12× 3	2 2	30× 5
5	5+ 2	1	4	7+ 3	6
18× 6	3	2	5 5	4	3− 1
6+ 3	6 6	8+ 5	2	1	4
2	1− 5	24× 4	1	6	3 3
1	4	2÷ 3	6	10× 5	2

247

2÷ 6	3	3+ 2	9+ 5	4	1 1
10× 5	2	1	5+ 4	3 3	18× 6
2÷ 2	20× 5	4 4	1	30× 6	3
1	4	9+ 3	6 6	5	7+ 2
3- 4	1	6	1- 3	2÷ 2	5
3 3	11+ 6	5	2	1	4 4

248

10+ 1	7+ 5	36× 3	2	6	4 4
4	2	11+ 6	5	3÷ 3	1
5	2- 3	1	10+ 6	4	13+ 2
1- 2	72× 6	4	3	2÷ 1	5
3	4- 1	5	5+ 4	2	6
6 6	2÷ 4	2	1	2- 5	3

249

9+ 2	20× 5	4	5- 1	6	3 3
1	1- 4	3	30× 6	7+ 5	2
6	2÷ 3	3- 2	5	4 4	3- 1
3 3	6	5	2÷ 2	1	4
24× 4	1	6	3 3	24× 2	11+ 5
7+ 5	2	1 1	4	3	6

250

3÷ 2	6	8+ 3	5+ 1	15+ 5	4
8× 4	2	5	3	1	6
1	3- 5	2	13+ 6	4	3
2- 3	1	96× 4	3÷ 2	6	6+ 5
11+ 5	12× 3	6	4	12× 2	1
6	4	4- 1	5	3	2